How?

Owlkids Books Inc.
10 Lower Spadina Avenue, Suite 400, Toronto, Ontario M5V 2Z2
www.owlkids.com

Distributed in Canada by University of Toronto Press
5201 Dufferin Street, Toronto, Ontario M3H 5T8

Distributed in the United States by Publishers Group West
1700 Fourth Street, Berkeley, California 94710

To my parents, who taught me to ask who, when, what, where, why, and how. And to my great friend
Kari Lynn Winters, who had the clever idea for a book called *How?* — S.R.

Library and Archives Canada Cataloguing in Publication

Ripley, Catherine, 1957-
    How? : the most awesome question and answer book about nature,
animals, people, places-- and you! / by Catherine Ripley ; illustrated by Scot Ritchie.

Includes index.
Issued also in electronic format.
ISBN 978-1-926973-24-1

    1. Children's questions and answers. I. Ritchie, Scot II. Title.

AG195.R57 2012   j031.02   C2011-905811-1

Library of Congress Control Number: 2011935953

Design: Barb Kelly

Canadian Heritage   Patrimoine canadien

Canada

Ontario
Ontario Media Development Corporation
Société de développement de l'industrie des médias de l'Ontario

Canada Council for the Arts   Conseil des Arts du Canada

ONTARIO ARTS COUNCIL
CONSEIL DES ARTS DE L'ONTARIO

We acknowledge the financial support of the Canada Council for the Arts, the Ontario Arts Council,
the Government of Canada through the Canada Book Fund (CBF) and the Government of Ontario
through the Ontario Media Development Corporation's Book Initiative for our publishing activities.

Manufactured by WKT Co. Ltd.
Manufactured in Shenzhen, Guangdong, China, in December 2011
Job #11CB2231

A   B   C   D   E   F

Publisher of Chirp, chickaDEE and OWL
www.owlkids.com

How?

The most awesome question and answer book about nature, animals, people, places—and you!

By Catherine Ripley
Illustrated by Scot Ritchie

Owl kids

List of Questions

Happy Birthday! 11

How did birthday parties get started? 14

How do balloons float? 16

Why do balloons pop? 18

Why do we have noisemakers?...........20

Why do we wrap presents? 22

How do I grow taller each year?..........24

How does batter turn into cake?..........26

Why do we sing the birthday song?.......28

How do candles stay on fire? 30

Why is cake so yummy? 32

Off to the Library 35

Who invented the library? 38

How does the library get all its books? 40

How are books made?....................42

Why are some books hardcover and some paperback? 44

Why do I need to be quiet in the library? ..46

Does reading make me smarter? 48

Why do libraries have computers? 50

How do computers know stuff? 52

How do librarians remember where all the books go?........................54

Does every library have a restroom? 56

What happens when I check out a book? ..58

Feeling Sick 87

How do I get sick? 90

Why do I throw up? 92

Why does the thermometer go
in my ear? 94

Why do I get a fever when I get sick? 96

How do I sneeze? 98

How do I catch somebody else's cold? ... 100

Why do I have to get lots of rest
when I'm sick? 102

When should I go to the doctor? 104

How is medicine made? 106

How does medicine work? 108

Pets, Pets, Pets! 61

Where do pets come from? 64

Why are dogs different sizes? 66

Do dogs dream? 68

Why do bettas fight? 70

How do fish see under water? 72

How come tarantulas are so hairy? 74

Why do cats purr? 76

How do parrots talk? 78

How do snakes eat really big stuff? 80

Why do hamsters go on a wheel? 82

Why do hamsters stuff their cheeks? 84

Road Trip

Road Trip 111

How does the steering wheel turn the car? 114

Why are there so many different traffic signs? . . 116

Why are wheels round? 118

How are roads built? 120

How are bridges built? 124

Why does gasoline smell so strong? 126

Why are there speed limits? 128

Why does it look like
there is water on the road ahead? 130

How come my sister gets carsick? 132

Who invented the first car? 134

At the Beach 137

How does the sand get so hot? 140

How does all the sand get to the beach? . 142

Why does wet sand work better
for sandcastles? 144

Why do beaches have seagulls? 146

How do shells get so shiny? 148

Why do I hear the sea in a shell? 150

How do I float in the water? 152

Why is the ocean salty? 154

How are waves made? 156

Why does the water knock over
my sandcastle? 158

How many whales are in the oceans? 160

Why does the Sun burn me? 162

Airport Good-byes 165

How do planes land so easily? 168

Who invented the airplane? 170

Why are airports so busy? 172

Why do you need a passport? 176

How do X-rays work? 178

Where does my suitcase go? 180

Why do hugs make you feel so good? 182

Why does the security gate beep? 184

How do planes take off when
they weigh so much? 186

Index 190

8

Happy Birthday!

13

How did birthday parties get started?

The invention of calendars helped. Long, long ago, people watched the changes of the Moon, the Sun, and the seasons to track time, so it was hard to remember the exact day someone was born. When calendars were invented about 6,000 years ago, remembering became much easier. But at first only the birthdays of kings or saints or heroes were celebrated. Then, about 150 years ago, ordinary people started celebrating their own birthdays. They also started paying more attention to children—and threw them birthday parties, too. Yahoo!

How do balloons float?

The balloons bobbing in the air at birthday parties are filled with a gas called helium. Helium makes balloons lighter than air, and whoosh, up they float! Like most gases, helium can't be seen, but it has weight and takes up space. In fact, it is the second-lightest gas of all and much lighter than air. No wonder a helium balloon will rise up, up, up—so hold on to that string!

When you fill a balloon with your breath, which is made up mainly of a gas called carbon dioxide, the balloon drops to the ground. That's because carbon dioxide is heavier than air.

Why do balloons pop?

Because they are snapping back to their original size! If you look at rubbery balloons under a microscope, you'll see long, stringy bits that are too small to see with your eyes. These stringy bits link up to hold the balloon together. As you blow up a balloon, all those long, stringy bits stretch…and stretch…and stretch. If you fill the balloon too much or poke a hole in it, the links between the strings break apart and the air rushes out.

Fibers

POP!

Why do we have noisemakers?

Today we use noisemakers for fun. But once upon a time, people made noise to protect the birthday person. That's because birthdays are times of change as a new year starts. People thought both bad and good spirits were around at such times. To keep the bad spirits away from the birthday person, friends and family stopped by to pass on their good wishes. And some people made lots of noise to scare away the bad spirits. One, two, three, blow!

Why do we wrap presents?

Because surprises are fun! And because wrapping makes gifts look extra special. Thanks to people in ancient China, paper has been around for more than 2,000 years. But it has only been about 120 years since printers first figured out how to print large rolls of sturdy, colored paper on their printing presses. Today, gifts are also wrapped in tea towels, cloth bags, old comics, and boxes. What's inside? Surprise!

How do I grow taller each year?

Inch by inch, cell by cell! How tall you will end up mostly depends on how tall your parents are. Until you reach your adult height, the number of cells in your body keeps increasing, and so you grow taller as you age. Usually, you grow the fastest as a baby. Most babies grow about 25 centimeters, or 10 inches, taller by the time they turn one. That's a lot of growing! Then you get a bit taller every year, sometimes in spurts, until eventually you stop growing. For some people, this happens around age 14, for others, sooner, and for still others, way later. It all depends!

How does batter turn into cake?

The combination of eggs, gas bubbles, and heat makes the change happen. First off are the eggs. Eggs help hold together the butter, sugar, and flour in the batter.

Second are the gas bubbles. Some are added through beating together the butter, eggs, and sugar. But most come from adding baking powder or baking soda. When these powders mix with certain liquids, a gas called carbon dioxide is given off. The result? Lots of bubbles!

Third, you need heat. The oven's heat makes the gas bubbles get bigger. It also makes the egg mixture solidify.

Ta-da! Cake!

Why do we sing the birthday song?

Because of two sisters named Patty and Mildred Hill. The sisters were teachers and lived in Louisville, Kentucky, in the United States. In 1893, they made up a song called "Good Morning to All" for their students. Around the 1920s, they changed the words but used the same tune. "Happy Birthday to You" was the result. Today the song has been translated into many languages and is sung around the world.

How do candles stay on fire?

The wax melts, turns into a gas, and feeds the flame. There are two parts to a wax candle: the wick and the wax. The wick is a special string found in the middle of the wax. When you light a candle, the match or lighter heats up the wick to the point where it bursts into flame. Then the heat of the fire starts to melt the nearby wax. As the wax melts, it becomes a liquid and is drawn up the wick. When the melted wax reaches the bottom of the flame, it feeds, or fuels, the flame. Poof! The liquid turns into a gas that burns with a bit of smoke! Flicker, flicker, flicker!

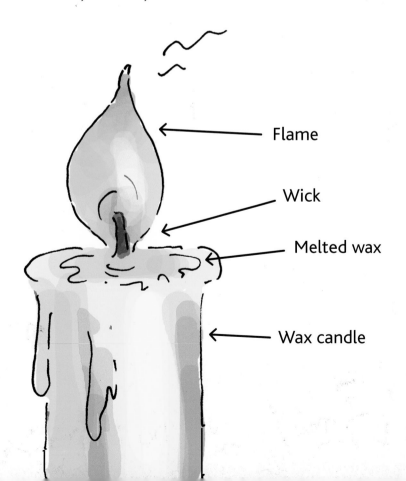

Flame

Wick

Melted wax

Wax candle

Why is cake so yummy?

Cake has lots and lots of sugar in it, and your body reads sugar as "yummy." Here's how it works: First, the cake smell rises to your nose. A message goes to your brain: "Smells like cake!" As you take a bite, your taste buds send a similar message to your brain: "Tastes like cake!" Your brain then decides whether the cake smell and taste are sour, savory, bitter, salty, or sweet. "Sweet!" Now, because your body needs a certain amount of high-energy sweet food to help you grow, the brain sends out the message: "Mmmm-mmm! Eat! Yummy!"

HAPPY BIRTHDAY!

My Party!

Cookie's birthday howls

Sweet piñata

Fire-hot balloon!

Time for cake. Yum!

It was a really FUN day!

Off to the Library

Who invented the library?

No one knows for sure! A library is an organized collection of writings and pictures, and today anyone can go to a public library. You can visit, either in person or online, to find information, read books and magazines, listen to stories, and borrow items.

But this wasn't always the case. Several thousand years ago, mainly kings and emperors owned and used libraries. Then, over many years, as more and more people learned how to read, libraries became a good idea for everyone, not just kings. Three cheers for everyone being able to go to a library!

Thousands of years ago, many books were clay tablets. Others were scrolls.

leview Library
TODAY
at the
Mapleview
Library
Story Time
10:00 a.m.

How does the library get all its books?

Sometimes books are given, or donated, to a library. And sometimes a library might borrow a book someone wants from another library. But libraries mostly buy their books. Librarians are the ones who get to choose new books—as well as music, magazines, movies, and online databases— for their libraries. They try to build a collection that covers many different subjects for the people who visit the library.

How do librarians choose what to buy? They keep on top of new things that are being published. They think about what is missing from their collections and about what people are asking for. What's new on the shelf today?

How are books made?

With the work of many, many people!

1 A book starts with an idea and a publisher who is willing to pay for turning the idea into a book.

2 An author writes the book, and an editor makes the writing as clear and correct as possible.

3 A designer decides what the book will look like. If artwork is needed, an artist or a photographer (or sometimes both) supplies it. The designer puts the words and pictures together on the pages.

4 A production manager decides who will print the book, figures out the costs, and orders the work to begin. The costs depend on if it is a paper, electronic, or audio book.

5 For a hardcover or paperback book, a printer prints all the pages, puts the pages in order, and binds the book together. A cover is added.

6 Ta-da! The books are ready to be shipped to libraries and bookstores.

Why are some books hardcover and some paperback?

Because different readers like different kinds of books! Hardcover books are sturdier and last longer. They're a good choice for libraries, where many, many people read the same book. Although paperbacks won't last as long, they are lighter and less expensive. And some books don't have covers at all. Audio books, for example, can be a good choice for people "on the go" or those who can't read very well. And e-books (electronic books) can be great if you have a computer or electronic reader handy.

Hardcover books are sturdier and last longer.

Paperbacks are lighter and cheaper.

Shhhhh

Why do I need to be quiet in the library?

It's the respectful thing to do. While conversation is welcomed in many libraries, and silence is not a must, being quiet is a sign of respect for other library users. The real question is: are you disturbing anyone? If you are speaking on the phone, laughing with friends, or listening to music so loudly that other people can't read or write easily, that could be a problem. A library staff member may ask you to lower your voice or your music. Think of others! Shhhh…

Does reading make me smarter?

Yes! Lots of scientists think so. Many scientists have studied people's brains, and they are able to see that reading helps the brain grow and change and learn. Reading is like exercise for your brain. The more reading you do, the stronger your brain gets. As you read, thoughts fill your mind. You learn new words and think about new ideas, and sometimes what you read makes you ask new questions. Without a doubt, reading lots and lots makes your brain grow stronger—and smarter!

Why do libraries have computers?

Computers help libraries help people. First, library computers connect people with the internet. This is especially important for those who don't have computers at home. Some children do their homework, play games, or chat with friends on the library computers. Also, computers let people look at the library catalog, which lists all the items available for borrowing—either in the building or from other libraries. Finally, computers help the library staff. Staff members use computers to keep track of all their items and library users, update their website, balance their budget, order new titles, answer questions from people, and check out books.

How do computers know stuff?

Because of people! Computers can't think for themselves yet. People create the information, or "stuff," a computer knows. And people, using a special computer language, tell the computer how to do the jobs they want it to do. This is called programming. For example, a computer programmer tells the computer how to check spelling, add up numbers, or find information.

Some information is stored right in a computer's memory or on a CD. But if you are connected to the internet, your computer talks with other computers to find the information you're looking for.

How do librarians remember where all the books go?

Through a system of call numbers. Call numbers are given to all library items. The first part of the number matches up with a certain section of the library. For example, storybook titles belong in the fiction section of the library, while information titles go in the nonfiction section. The second part of the number gives each title its own special spot within that section.

This call number says this book about hamsters is for children (J) and belongs in the Pets (636) section.

Library users and librarians can use the call number to track down where the title is. And each item can be put back into its right place every time so anyone can find it.

Does every library have a restroom?

Yup! Pretty much. Most libraries are pubic buildings, or they are in public buildings, which are usually required to have restrooms. The number of restrooms depends on how big the building is or how many people the library is designed to welcome. The more people who are expected to use the building, the more "water closets" (or toilets) are needed! Public restrooms usually have at least one stall that works for someone who is disabled.

What happens when I check out a book?

The checkout system makes a record of who is borrowing what. Each book or other item you borrow has a bar code or a computer chip. When scanned, the item is then linked to all sorts of information in the computer, such as what the item is and which library it is from.

Your library card also has a bar code or a chip. Again, this acts like a key to the information you have given the library—your name, address, and phone number.

At the checkout, both the item and your card are scanned, and an electronic record is made. The record links you to the item you have borrowed as well as to the date the item is due back. This way, the library always knows where its materials are.

LIBRARY VISIT

My own
library card

Story time

Lizzie's new book

Learning about
hamsters on
the internet

I ♥
BOOKS

Pets, Pets, Pets!

Where do pets come from?

From all over the place! Wherever you go to choose a pet, it's a good idea to ask where it comes from, how it will fit into your daily life, and how to take good care of it.

Some pets may come from neighbors who are raising animals such as guinea pigs, dogs, budgies, or fish.

Some may come from animal shelters, which are always working to find new homes for hurt or homeless animals.

And of course, many pets come from pet stores. Stores may raise some of the pets they sell, and many buy animals from breeders living in your home area. Stores also buy animals such as rare fish or reptiles from breeders farther away.

Why are dogs different sizes?

Different dogs for different folks! From the tiny Chihuahua to the giant Great Dane, dogs have many shapes, sizes, and special traits that have been bred into them by people over thousands of years. People watch for dogs with a special trait, such as small size. Then they breed these dogs together so that the wanted trait repeats and is strengthened in the new batch of puppies—and their puppies' puppies, and so on.

The tiny, silky-haired Yorkshire terrier was originally bred to kill rats in English factories in the 1800s.

OFF-LEASH AREA

The long-legged Afghan hound was bred for speed as a hunting dog.

Do dogs dream?

Yup! Scientists think so. Like you, dogs go through different stages of sleep each night. The first stage is called quiet sleep. During this stage, a dog breathes slowly and regularly, her heartbeat slows down, and it's easy to wake her up.

Next comes something called active sleep. Now the dog's breathing speeds up, her eyes flutter, and her brain is busy. During active sleep, a dog might twitch or move her legs or even yelp. Scientists believe this activity is a sure sign that dogs are dreaming.

Why do bettas fight?

To protect their territory! But guess what? Bettas only fight with other bettas, not with other types of fish. In Southeast Asia, wild "fighting fish" bettas mainly live in the still, shallow water of huge rice fields. Here, each fish tries to claim some territory so it can mate and have babies. The female betta lays the eggs, but the male takes care of them. First he blows a bubble nest. Then he picks up the eggs and places them in the nest. Until the baby bettas hatch a few days later, he protects the nest. Watch out, other bettas!

How do fish see under water?

Near the top of a lake or ocean, where there is lots of light, fish use their eyes to see. Their eyes are shaped differently than your eyes and see perfectly under water. Plus, a clear covering protects their open eyes all the time. No diving masks required! But deep in the ocean, where it is dark, dark, dark, fish "see" in other ways. They use special cells along their sides and on their heads. These cells let fish "see" by feeling anything that is moving nearby. Some fish even "see" by smelling or using their whiskers!

Blossom

SAMMY

How come tarantulas are so hairy?

All the better to touch, taste, and feel the world around them, and also to protect themselves. All spiders have hairs, but tarantulas are the hairiest of all. Many of their hairs make them extra-sensitive to any movement or vibration—a good thing, as tarantulas can't see well and are up and about at night. Thanks to their hairs, they can quickly tell if some food is walking by their burrow or if danger is near. Some tree-climbing tarantulas have special hairs on their feet that help them stick to smooth leaves. And one type of tarantula rubs its leg hairs together to "hiss" at enemies and frighten them away. Still others flick special barbed hairs at their enemies. Ouch!

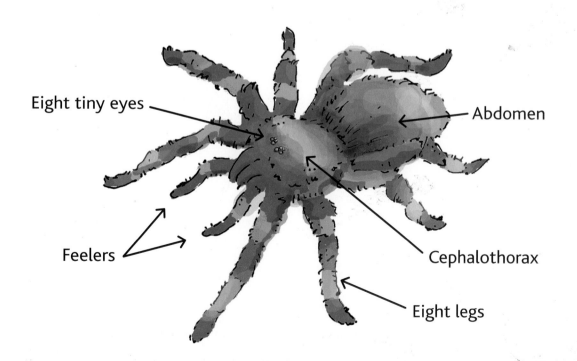

Eight tiny eyes

Abdomen

Feelers

Cephalothorax

Eight legs

Why do cats purr?

Most often, purring is a sign that cats are purr-fectly happy. Cats purr when they are being stroked or petted, and newborn kittens purr when they are nursing. But sometimes cats purr when they are hurt or scared. Some scientists think purring may help cats calm themselves down, and so they are asking: is purring a cat's way of getting better and staying healthy? Maybe. Amazingly, some scientists have found that certain soft, steady, rumbly sounds, like purring, seem to help heal cats' illnesses and help their bones grow strong.

Purrrr

How do parrots talk?

They are copycats! Like most birds, parrots have something called a syrinx deep in their throats, just where the windpipe goes into their lungs. Air traveling in and out of the lungs goes through the syrinx. This makes the syrinx vibrate, or quiver, and the vibrations make the sounds. A parrot's secret is that it has super control over how much air flows through the syrinx. It also has a fatter tongue than most birds, which helps it shape sounds more easily. Add these two things together with the parrot's great hearing, its love of repeating whatever it hears, and its intelligence, and what do you get? Polly wants a cracker!

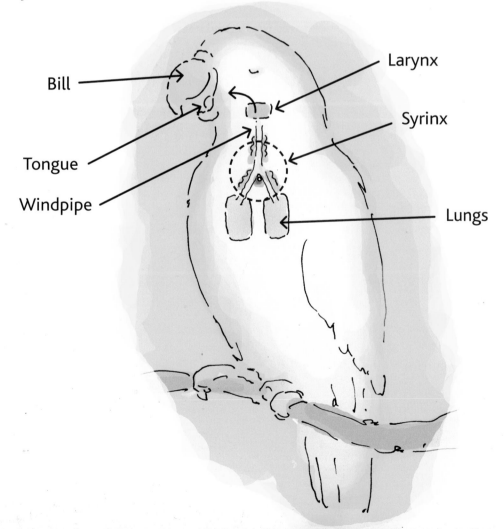

Bill

Tongue

Windpipe

Larynx

Syrinx

Lungs

How do snakes eat really big stuff?

They have special teeth and jaws that can open super wide. Your jaws are firmly attached to your skull. A snake's aren't! Instead, stretchy ligaments join a snake's jaws to its skull. And while your jaws can't move totally apart at the back of your mouth, a snake's can! To top it off, a snake's bottom jaw is split in two at the front. Each side can move on its own, which is great for pulling in food bit by bit by bit. And finally, a snake's teeth all point backward, which is a huge help for gulping down a giant-sized meal.

Why do hamsters go on a wheel?

Lots of running keeps pet hamsters happy and healthy! In the wild, hamsters are used to being on the move. Because they live in deserts and scrubby areas in Asia and parts of Europe, they often have to travel a long way to find food. They also dig deep, deep burrows for their homes. In a cage, hamsters can't move around as freely. A wheel lets a pet hamster have a super workout every day, whenever it's ready to go, go, go!

Some hamsters can run up to several miles each day on their wheels.

Why do hamsters stuff their cheeks?

To carry home as much food as possible! As a pet, a hamster doesn't need to worry about where its next meal is coming from, but in the wild, it does. To survive long, cold winters, a hamster stashes away roots, seeds, nuts, and grains in its underground home. For this job, its "backpack" cheek pouches are great! They let the hamster travel far from home and collect food at the same time. The cheek pouches, which are dry inside, get bigger and bigger until they are full. Then it's time to head for home!

Mapleview Pet Expo

Goldfish named **Bubbles!**

Time for a snooze

Hammy has a snack

Making a slithery friend

Dogs are my fave!

Feeling Sick

How do I get sick?

It all has to do with germs. Germs are microbes—tiny living things that are too small to see without a microscope. While some microbes are helpful, such as the ones that live in your tummy and help digest your food, germ microbes make you sick. Like all microbes, germs are always trying to multiply, or make more of themselves, to keep living. When germs move into your body and start multiplying—FAST—your body fights back. You run a fever, which helps fight off the germs. But it sure makes you feel yucky. Sniffle! Cough! *Ah-choo*!

Why do I throw up?

It's your body's way of protecting you. Usually the juices in your stomach and intestines can kill any bacteria or viruses that get into them. But if there are way too many, or if it is a very strong, bad germ, a message goes to your brain: "Danger! Something bad here!" And your brain answers, "Get rid of it!" Then your intestine and stomach muscles push any food inside back up and out. Blech! All gone! You're left with a super-yucky smell, a bad headache, and a sore tummy. For some people, a rollercoaster ride or car ride are other times when the brain senses things aren't right. For protection, their brains say "Barf!" and so they do.

Two types of germs, bacteria and viruses, cause most of the common illnesses everyone gets.

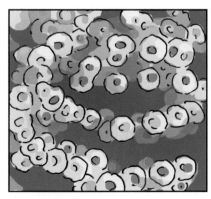

Bacteria can cause sicknesses like earaches and strep throat.

Viruses can cause sicknesses like colds and flu.

Why does the thermometer go in my ear?

So it can record how much heat your inner ear is giving off. This lets your mom or dad know what your body temperature is. Finding out is important because if your temperature is too high or too low, it's usually a sign that something is not quite right in your body. Some thermometers can read your skin temperature, but they are not as accurate as an ear thermometer or other types of thermometers that go inside your body. Whether they're placed in your mouth, bum, or ear, these thermometers give your mom or dad, doctor or nurse, a better reading as to how hot you really are.

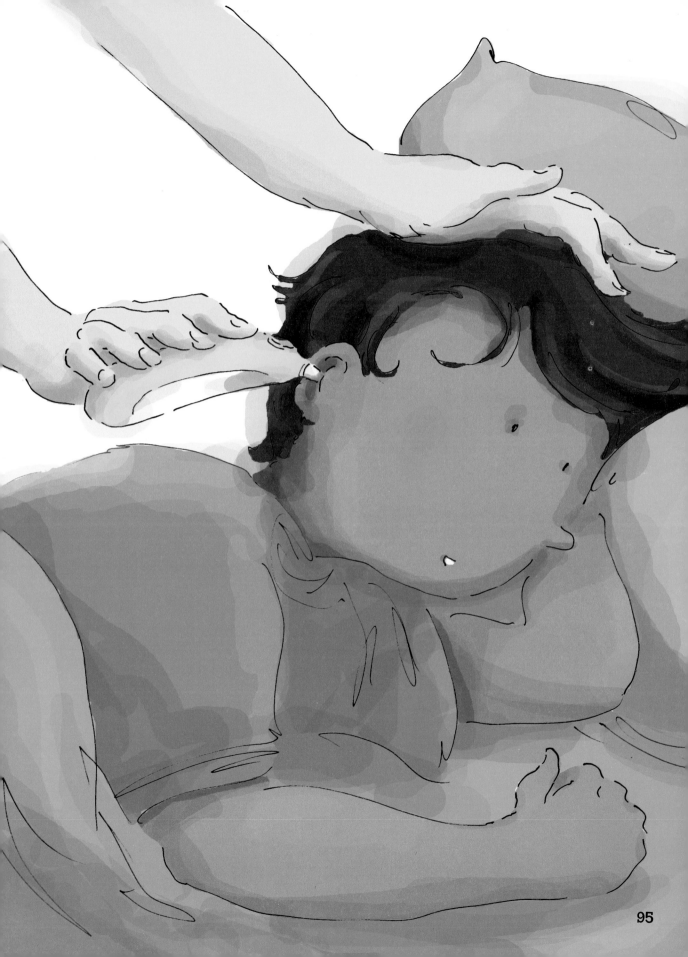

Why do I get a fever when I get sick?

So you will get better faster. A hot body temperature helps kill off the germs making you sick or stops them from multiplying. When your body is fighting germs, messages go to your brain, telling it to turn up the heat. You may also start to shiver. When you shiver, your muscles tighten and relax, tighten and relax...very, very quickly. All this extra muscle movement warms up your body even faster. Up, up goes your temperature. Once your body reaches the right "germ-fighting" temperature, the shivering stops. And once the germs are under control, your temperature goes back down. Phew!

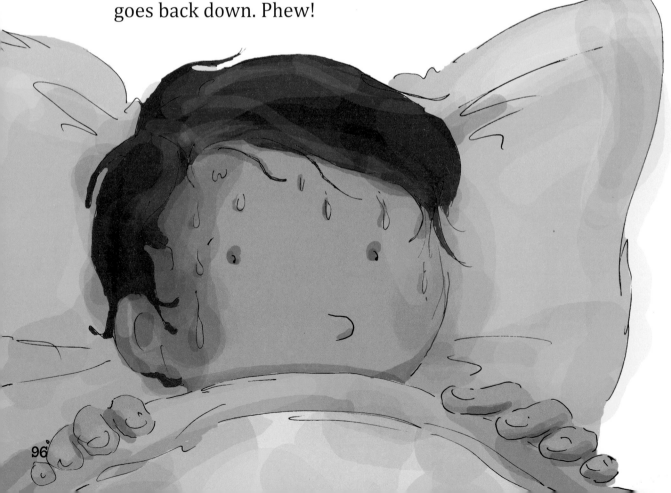

Normal body
temperature

Germs

When your body
turns up the heat, it
weakens bad germs.

How do I sneeze?

Your brain gets muscles from different parts of your body working together to ah-choo out whatever is tickling your nose. Pollen, dust, pepper, or nose slime can all trigger a sneeze. Whatever the reason, your muscles need to work together in just the right order to get rid of the tickle.

Ahhhh-
choooo!

First, the big muscle above your tummy helps you breathe in an extra-big breath of air... *AHHHHH*... Then your stomach, chest, and throat muscles blast out the air from your lungs in one big burst...*CHOOOO!* Even your eyelid muscles squeeze tight. Tickle gone!

How do I catch somebody else's cold?

Either by breathing in germs that are floating in the air or by touching something with another person's germs on it. That's why it's so very, very important to wash your hands LOTS so you can help stop cold germs from getting inside your body.

If your friend sneezes or coughs into the air instead of into her arm, tiny droplets spray out. If you are nearby, you might breathe in the droplets, which are full of cold germs, from the air.

If you are not nearby, you might still pick up the germs by touching something the droplets have landed on, such as a toy.

Now if you touch your mouth, eyes, or nose with your hand—uh-oh! You are on your way to getting your friend's cold.

Why do I have to get lots of rest when I'm sick?

Fighting cold or flu germs takes lots of energy, and resting helps your body focus its energy on getting healthy again. If you are using your energy to run or bike or catch a ball, you make it harder for your body to get better. When you are sick, your brain sends more blood to body parts that need fixing, such as your throat. Your nose and mouth make extra-slimy mucus so that germs slide out with the mucus when you cough or sneeze. Your body is also making special germ-fighting cells that can stick to the cold or flu germs or "eat" them. It's a lot of hard work. Resting sure helps!

When should I go to the doctor?

At least once a year for a regular checkup! A yearly visit lets your doctor keep track of how you are growing, answer your questions, and chat with your mom or dad about your health. But your mom or dad should also call or take you to a doctor if you are sick and you seem to be getting worse.

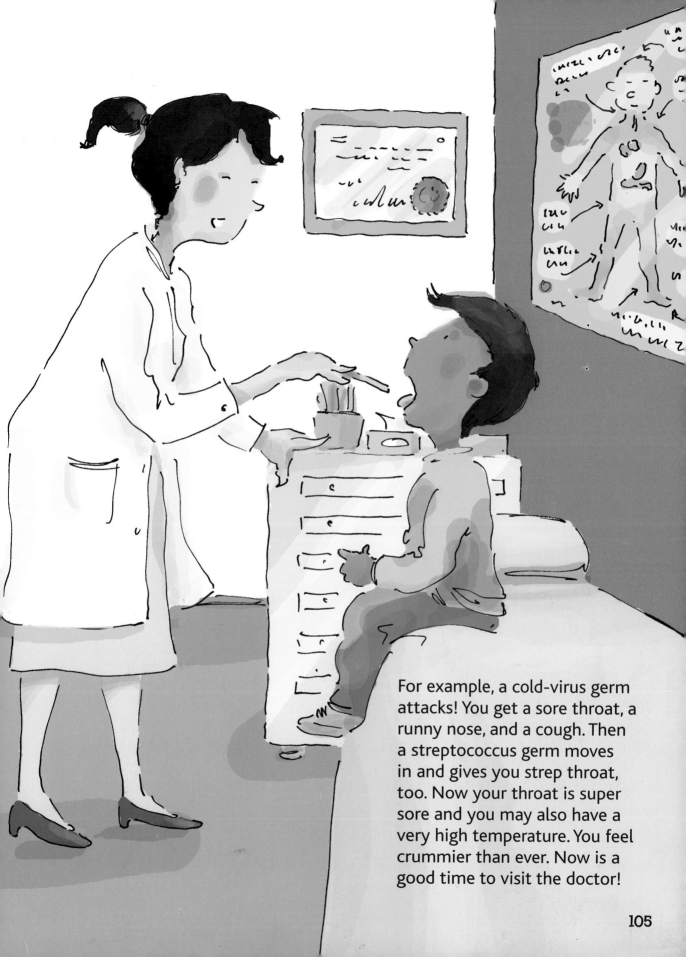

For example, a cold-virus germ attacks! You get a sore throat, a runny nose, and a cough. Then a streptococcus germ moves in and gives you strep throat, too. Now your throat is super sore and you may also have a very high temperature. You feel crummier than ever. Now is a good time to visit the doctor!

How is medicine made?

Very, very carefully! Making medicine is like baking a cake. You need to mix the right ingredients in the right amounts in just the right way. Many ingredients come from things found in nature, such as salt, plants, or microbes. Scientists make and test medicines in places called laboratories. They ask questions such as: Is this mixture safe for people to swallow? How much is safe for a baby? Is it safe to take this medicine for a long time? It takes lots and lots of testing to answer all the questions before a new medicine arrives in the pharmacy for you to buy.

How does medicine work?

In four main ways: Some medicines help your body fight the germs that are making you sick. For example, medicines called antibiotics attack bacteria germs and stop them from making more of themselves. Other medicines make you feel better while your body heals itself. A common medicine called acetaminophen can bring down your fever. Still other medicines can help with a problem your body keeps having. If you have asthma, an inhaler can help you breathe more easily whenever you have an asthma attack. And finally, some medicines stop you from getting sick in the first place. The chicken pox vaccine can help keep you from getting chicken pox. You should take medicine only when an adult is present.

FEELING SICK

Getting my temperature taken

Oma read to me...LOTS!

Being sick is no fun!

Puzzle book from Lizzie

Resting on the couch with puppy

Road Trip

How does the steering wheel turn the car?

The secret lies in a special part under the car called the pinion gear. Gears work by passing along energy or movement to something else, and that's exactly what the pinion gear does. When the driver turns the steering wheel to the right, the pinion gear moves in a circle to the right. As it does, the gear's special teeth connect with grooves on a metal rod called the rack. The moving pinion gear gets the rack moving sideways and to the right. And because the rack connects to the wheels, the wheels follow along and the car turns right.

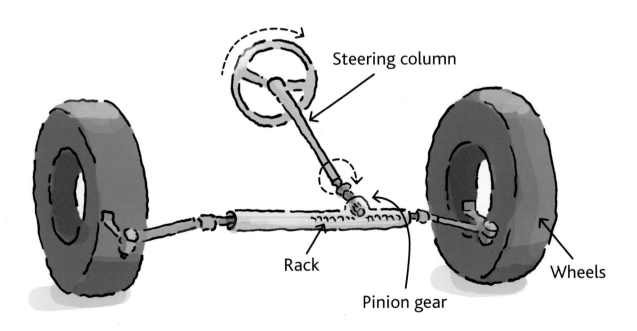

Steering column

Rack

Pinion gear

Wheels

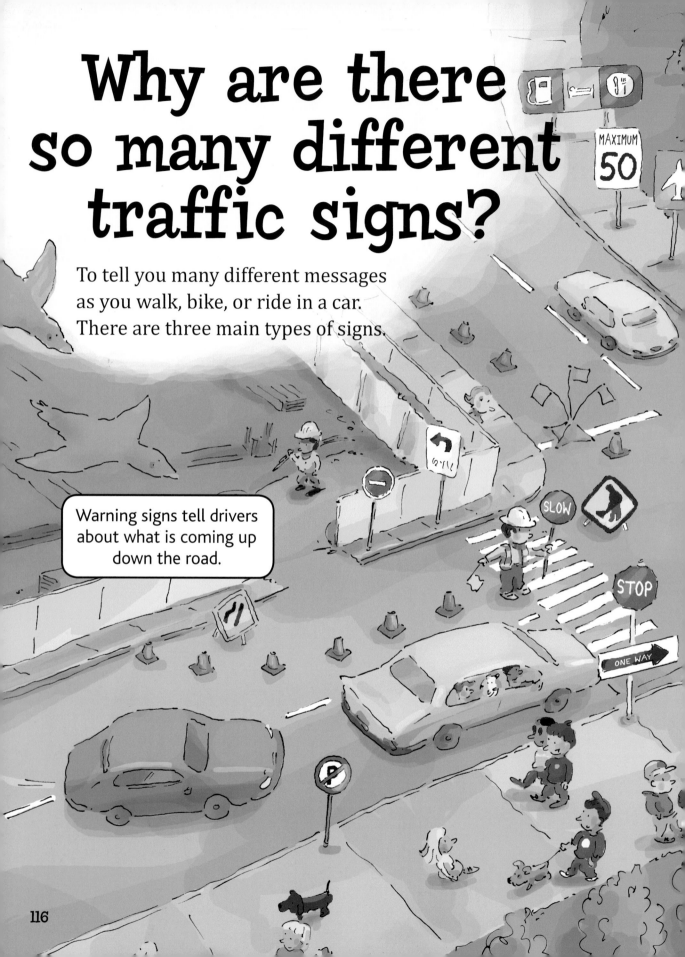

Why are there so many different traffic signs?

To tell you many different messages as you walk, bike, or ride in a car. There are three main types of signs.

Warning signs tell drivers about what is coming up down the road.

Information signs tell you about places to visit or services you might want to use.

Other signs tell you what you must do to stay safe.

7

Why are wheels round?

Because round things roll, and this makes moving people or things from place to place so much easier. Think about trying to push or pull a kid in a box along the sidewalk. Hard, eh? Now think about pushing or pulling a kid in a wagon. Easy! As the wagon rolls along, only a small part of each wheel touches the ground at any one time. This means there is much less of the sidewalk to "resist," or stop the wagon from moving forward. For moving heavy objects, the wheel is one of the most important inventions of all time. Keep on rolling!

How are roads built?

One step at a time!

Step 1: Road engineers make a plan. How many cars or trucks will use the road? Where will it go? How many bridges are needed?

Step 3: Sometimes big dips need to be filled with extra earth.

Step 4: Graders and compactors flatten the base to make it smooth.

Step 2: Earthmovers clear a path. Away with the rocks, trees, and topsoil!

Step 5: Workers might add cement so the base won't crumble.

Step 6: Dump trucks add gravel to the base. Now more flattening! More smoothing!

Step 8: If the road is asphalt, a big roller smooths it out. Three or four layers are usually needed.

Step 9: Lines and markings are painted to show cars the edge of the road, when they can pass, and so on.

Step 7: A surface layer of concrete or asphalt makes the road smooth and sturdy.

The new road is ready to go! VROOOM!

How are bridges built?

From the bottom up! To build a beam bridge, which is what most highway bridges are, strong foundations are a must. Next, the start and end points of the bridge, called abutments, and the big pillars in the middle, called piers, are built on top of the foundations. Steel or concrete beams are then lifted into place to join the ends. Now the roadway, or deck, which is usually made out of concrete strengthened with steel rods, is built over the beams. All done!

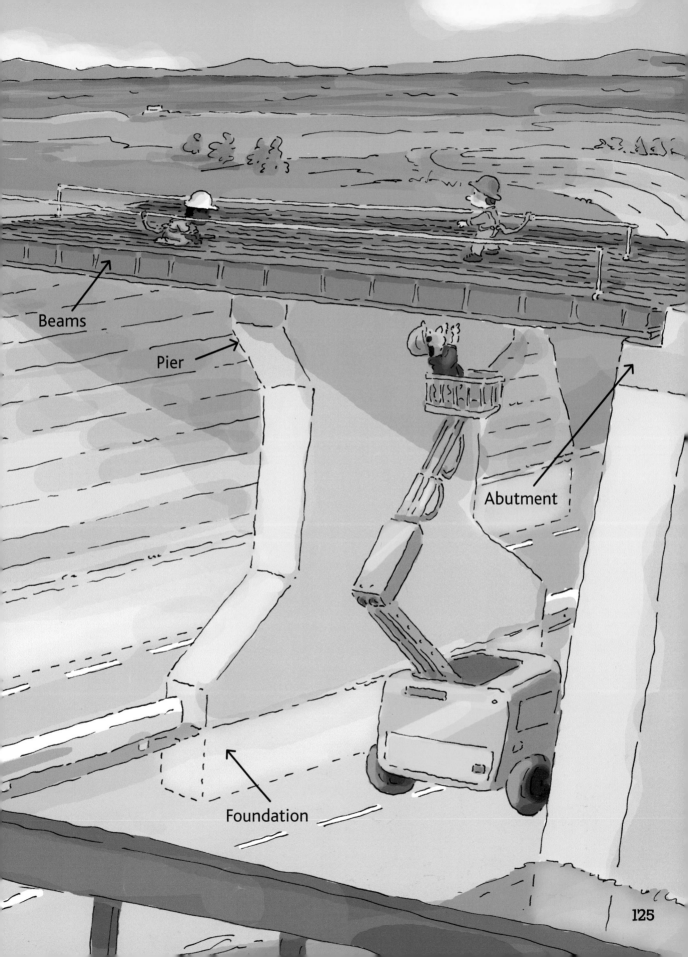

Beams

Pier

Abutment

Foundation

Why does gasoline smell so strong?

Because gasoline contains a liquid called benzene. And one of the most noticeable things about benzene is its strong, "sweet" smell. Gasoline can be dangerous if it leaks. It's poisonous and can light on fire very easily. So if there is a gasoline spill, people need to clean it up right away. The strong benzene smell is useful because it warns people that there's gasoline around. In contrast, the natural gas that is used to heat many homes has no smell. Like car gasoline, it is also dangerous, so an ingredient that smells like rotten eggs is added. It acts as a good warning signal for people, just as benzene does.

Why are there speed limits?

To keep everyone safe and the traffic flowing smoothly. Traffic engineers, people who set the speed limits, look at who is using the road. Is it just cars and trucks, or are people walking on sidewalks nearby? They also look at the type of road it is and where the road goes. Setting a high, or fast, speed on an expressway is okay, but a slower speed is safer for a narrow neighborhood street or a curvy mountain road. Sometimes lower speed limits are set for environmental reasons. The slower you go, the less gas the car uses, which creates less pollution. Yeah!

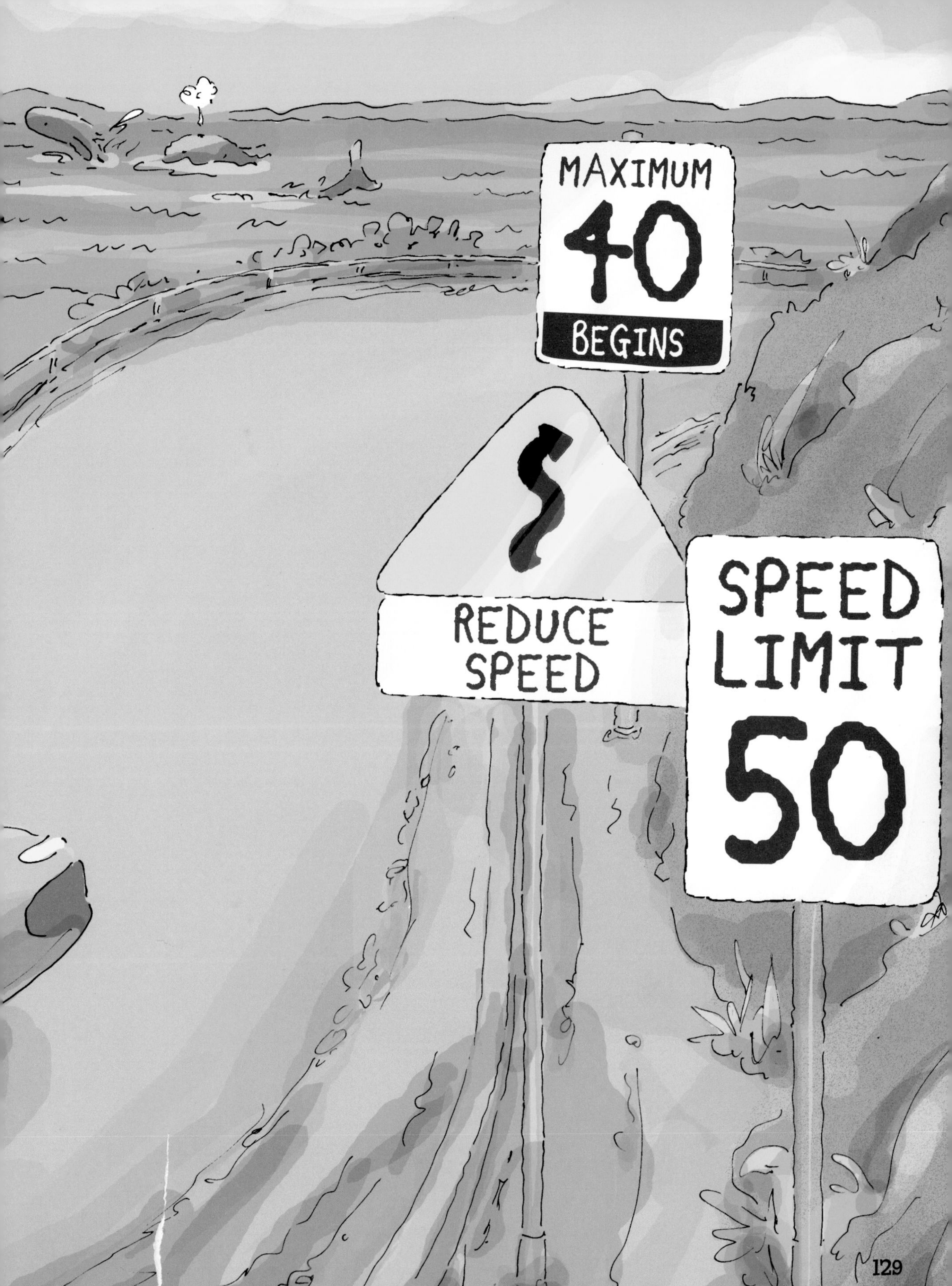
MAXIMUM
40
BEGINS
REDUCE
SPEED
SPEED
LIMIT
50

Why does it look like there is water on the road ahead?

Because on a sunny day, a layer of hot, thin air has built up over the road. Here's why the hot air makes a difference.

Light waves from the Sun and sky normally travel to Earth in straight lines. When the light rays, which are made up of all the colors of the rainbow, hit the road, some are absorbed and some bounce off. Ta-da, a black road is what we see!

But when it's sunny, a layer of air heats up just above the road and becomes very thin. Now when light rays travel toward the road, they hit this layer of hotter, thinner air. And guess what! This air makes the light rays bend upward. They bend upward so much that even though the road is still there, we don't see it. Instead we see a mirage! It looks as if there is shimmering water on the road— even though there is no water there at all!

How come my sister gets carsick?

Her brain is confused! Her eyes, ears, nose, and skin are always sensing things about the world around her. They also send messages to her brain about what is going on. Her eyes see houses and trees as the car drives past and her body feels the car moving. When all the senses send the same message, the brain thinks everything is fine. But if your sister can't see out the window, or if she is playing a game or reading a book, her eyes might be sending a different "I am still" message to her brain than the messages her other senses are sending. Now her brain is getting two different messages. Uh-oh! Her brain gets confused, and your sister feels sick or dizzy.

Who invented the first car?

Lots of people played a part, but big credit must go to Nicolas Cugnot of France. Here's why: Once upon a time, if people wanted to go somewhere by land and didn't want to walk, they hooked up an animal to a cart or sled, and off they went. In 1769, Nicolas Cugnot changed that. He invented a steam-powered tractor. No horses, husky dogs, or oxen required! Even though his giant tractor was nothing like the cars of today, it was a self-powered vehicle, and that was a great start. Putt, putt! Vroom, vroom! ZOOM!

Nicolas Cugnot's steam tractor, 1769

ROAD TRIP

Wheels everywhere!

Cool job building a bridge

Trucks at work

Lots to see on the road.

At the Beach

139

How does the sand get so hot?

Sand is a super-duper heat trap, especially when it's dry. When the Sun's rays hit the sand, they—along with the heat inside them—are taken into the sand, or absorbed. As long as the Sun is shining, the top layers of sand keep trapping more and more heat. Yikes!

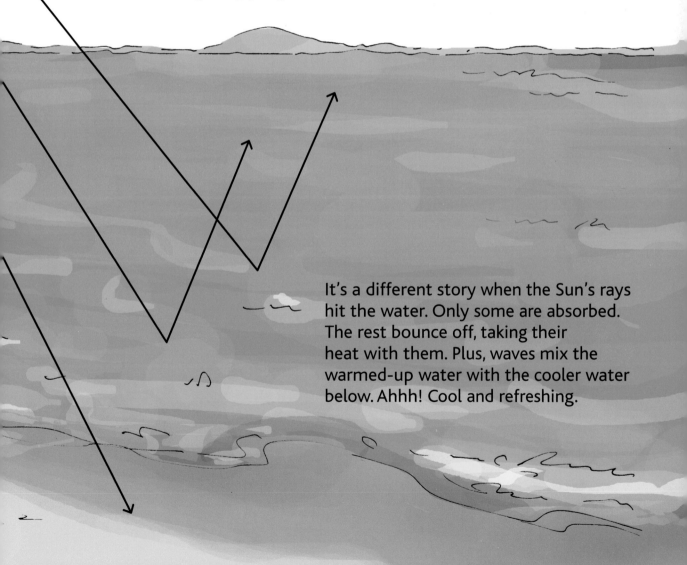

It's a different story when the Sun's rays hit the water. Only some are absorbed. The rest bounce off, taking their heat with them. Plus, waves mix the warmed-up water with the cooler water below. Ahhh! Cool and refreshing.

How does all the sand get to the beach?

It travels there by water and sometimes by wind! Rivers and streams flow from faraway inland places to the ocean. Along the way, sand gets picked up and whooshed along, too. Ocean waves then swirl the sand to the shore, leaving lots behind on the beach. Waves also bring sand from nearby. As the wind and rain pound on the ocean's rocky cliffs or banks, tiny, tiny bits break off and make new sand. Strong winds can also blow sand from one spot to another.

Sand is mainly made up of eensy, weensy pieces of rock, shell, or coral.

Why does wet sand work better for sandcastles?

Because water acts like glue. The outside surface of dry sand grains is smooth and hard. And smooth, hard things don't stick together well. But when you pour water on dry sand, it surrounds, or coats, each grain of sand. Because water is always trying to join up with other water, it sticks the grains of sand together. Sticky sand holds together really well, so now you can sculpt the sand into any shape you wish. Yay!

Why do beaches have seagulls?

Because beaches are safe places for gulls. With their bright white feathers, seagulls are easily seen by foxes, falcons, eagles, and other predators. But the wide-open spaces on a beach let seagulls spot these hungry hunters from afar. Meanwhile, they can digest what they've eaten, smooth their feathers, and keep an eye on other gulls. If a gull dives for a fish out at sea, the other gulls on the beach fly out, hoping to share. Plus, as the tide rolls in and out, new clams, crabs, and other creatures are left on the wet sand to snack on. Bonus!

147

How do shells get so shiny?

Because of something called the mantle. Mantles are found in a group of animals called mollusks, most of which live in shells. The mantle is like a wall between the animal's soft body and its hard outer shell. Its job is to keep making and repairing the shell as the animal grows. In some mollusks, such as clams, oysters, and mussels, the mantle is found only on the inside of the shell. In others, such as cowries, the mantle also wraps around the outside of the shell. Whatever part the mantle covers becomes shiny and oh so pretty!

Why do I hear the sea in a shell?

Whoosh, whoosh, whoosh! It may sound like wind and waves, but it's actually the echoes of the noises around you. Sounds—like traffic, laughter, or wind—travel to your ear in invisible waves. When you hold a shell to your ear, the sound waves do not enter your ear directly. They get caught up inside the shell first, bouncing back and forth off the inner walls. The sounds become muddled and no longer seem like themselves. Instead they sound like the sea!

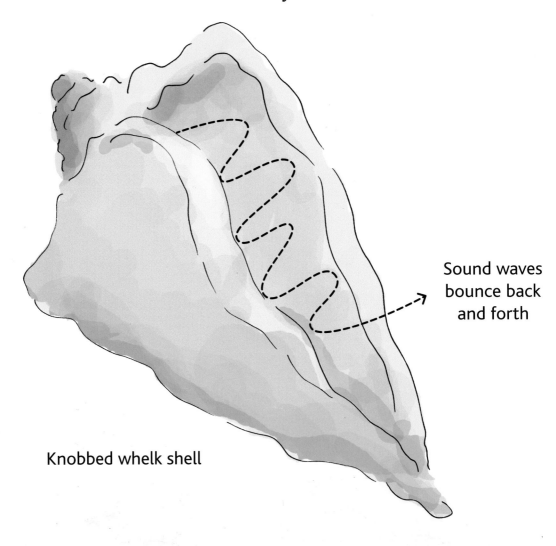

Sound waves bounce back and forth

Knobbed whelk shell

How do I float in the water?

Spreading out your body helps. Here's why: When you are trying to float, a force called gravity is trying to pull you down. At the same time, another force, called buoyancy, is trying to push you up. The more air you have in your lungs and the more body fat you have, the more buoyant you are. So when you spread out your body in the water, your lungs have more room to open up. This lets you breathe in more air, which makes your lungs act like air-filled balloons. Now the force of buoyancy is stronger than the force of gravity. Ta-da! You float.

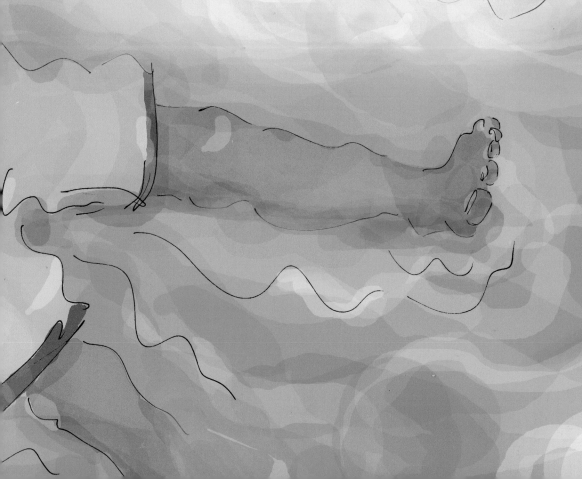

Why is the ocean salty?

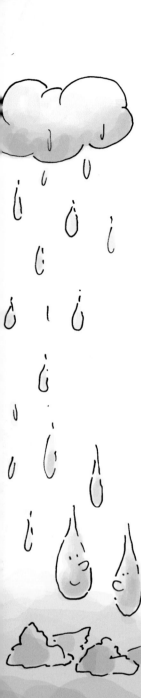

Because the world has lots of salt in it, and lots of it ends up in the ocean. Salt is made up of two ingredients: sodium and chlorine. Many rocks on land have sodium in them. Rain and rivers wash tiny bits of sodium from these rocks down to the ocean. Meanwhile, deep under the ocean, burning hot rocks and gases from inside the Earth seep or explode into the water. One of the gases is called chlorine. It joins up with the sodium in the water to make salt. Finally, some of the ocean water is always going into the air as a gas called water vapor. When it does, the salty part stays in the water. The result? Salty seas!

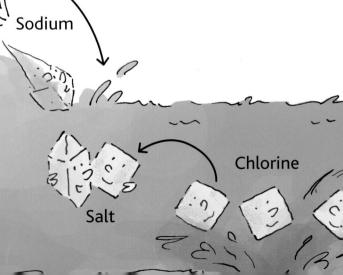

Sodium

Chlorine

Salt

How are waves made?

Mainly by the wind. When the wind blows over the water, some of its power, or energy, is passed to the water. This energy now pushes forward through the water as a wave. If the wind is a baby breeze, it makes small ripples. But a big wind can turn the ripples into giant waves. While the wind makes most waves, other things can cause them, too. Currents, which are paths of moving ocean, lake, or river water, can also make waves. And so can underwater earthquakes and landslides, or even boats sailing by!

Why does the water knock over my sandcastle?

You must have built your castle between the low- and high-tide marks! Every day, twice a day, oceans rise up the beaches of the world and then fall back down. This rise-and-fall movement is called the tide. High tide happens when the ocean creeps so far up the beach that water covers most of it. Low tide happens when the ocean goes back, leaving much of the beach uncovered. So if you build your sandcastle when the ocean is falling back to the low-tide mark, it is bound to get washed away when the ocean rises back up to the high-tide mark. Bye, bye, castle!

Tides happen mainly because of the Moon. The Moon is big and close enough to the Earth that it pulls on the Earth and its oceans, making the oceans bulge toward it.

Earth

Moon

Sun

Low tide

At the same time, because the Earth is spinning, water on the opposite side of the Earth also bulges out. Wherever the water bulges, it's high tide. The waters in between are at low tide. The Sun also pulls on the Earth and its oceans. When the Sun and Moon are pulling in the same direction, you get even higher tides.

How many whales are in the oceans?

No one really knows for sure. Counting whales is a challenge because they spend so much time under water, out of sight. Plus, they are always on the move. But scientists believe there are at least 87 different kinds of whales, or species, in the whale family, which includes whales, dolphins, and porpoises. And they believe that almost 20 species are in serious trouble. These species have been hunted too much, have been killed by fishing nets, or have had their ocean homes ruined by pollution or other human activities. Thankfully, many people are working hard to protect whales, dolphins, and porpoises from harm!

Why does the Sun burn me?

Because you've stayed out in the sunlight too long without protecting your skin. Sunlight is partly made up of invisible ultraviolet rays, called UV rays, and it is UV-B rays that burn your skin. Fortunately, a special substance in your skin, called melanin, protects you. But only to a certain point! If you stay out in the sunlight too long, the melanin can't protect your skin fully from the UV-B rays. Ouch! That's why it's a good idea to put on sunscreen and wear hats and other clothes that protect your skin, like long-sleeved shirts.

HITTING THE BEACH

Lizzie's sandcastle

Whale watching

Collecting shells

Catching some waves with Mom

Fun in the sun!

Airport Good-byes

DEPARTURES
I'll be back soon.
I wish you could stay, Oma.
Or maybe we'll come visit you!

How do planes land so easily?

It takes lots and lots of practice to land at just the right spot and at just the right speed every time—whether it's sunny, snowy, or sleety. If flying into a big airport, the pilot first asks to land and finds out which runway to use. After all, nobody wants two planes trying to land in the same place! Then the pilot lines up the plane with the runway and starts slowing it down. The landing gear goes down, too. Slowly and steadily, the pilot steers the plane down, down, down toward the runway. Easy does it...bump! Another perfect landing!

When a plane flies slower, there is less "lift," which makes it start to go down.

First Flight
Kitty Hawk, North Carolina, USA
December 17, 1903

Who invented the airplane?

Orville and Wilbur Wright—with help from other people who came before them. For years, people tried to build flying machines with wings that flapped like a bird's. Then a man named George Cayley asked, "What if we copied gliding birds instead? What if the power to go forward didn't come from flapping?" Over the next hundred years, people worked on engine ideas, wing shape, and a frame light enough to get off the ground but strong enough to carry a person and an engine. The Wright brothers put all the best ideas together. And they made it possible to control the plane. Eureka! A plane!

Why are airports so busy?

Because lots and lots of people want to fly to faraway places! Imagine being in one of the world's busiest airports and seeing 250,000 passengers travel through each day. That's enough people to fill a city. Wow! That means lots of planes are taking off and landing all day long—and at night, too. With the planes come lots of passengers and loads of cargo such as mail, equipment, even fresh fish. Lots of people work at the airport to help all those passengers, to fly the planes, and to handle the cargo.

CAFÉ

ARRIVALS

FOOD COURT

Turn the page to see how it all works...

175

It's always busy at the airport!

Fuel truck drivers deliver fuel to the planes.

Security gua— work to ke— everyone s—

Boarding area

Boarding gate agents welcome passengers.

Ramp agents load and unload suitcases.

Planes can't back up so *tug drivers* push the planes backward.

Flight attendants help passengers during their flight.

Runway

Lav truck drivers take the plane's toilet waste to a special disposal area.

Pilots fly the planes.

Flight tower

Air traffic controllers organize how planes land and take off.

People in administration hire workers, pay the bills, organize how the airlines use the airport, and keep everything running smoothly.

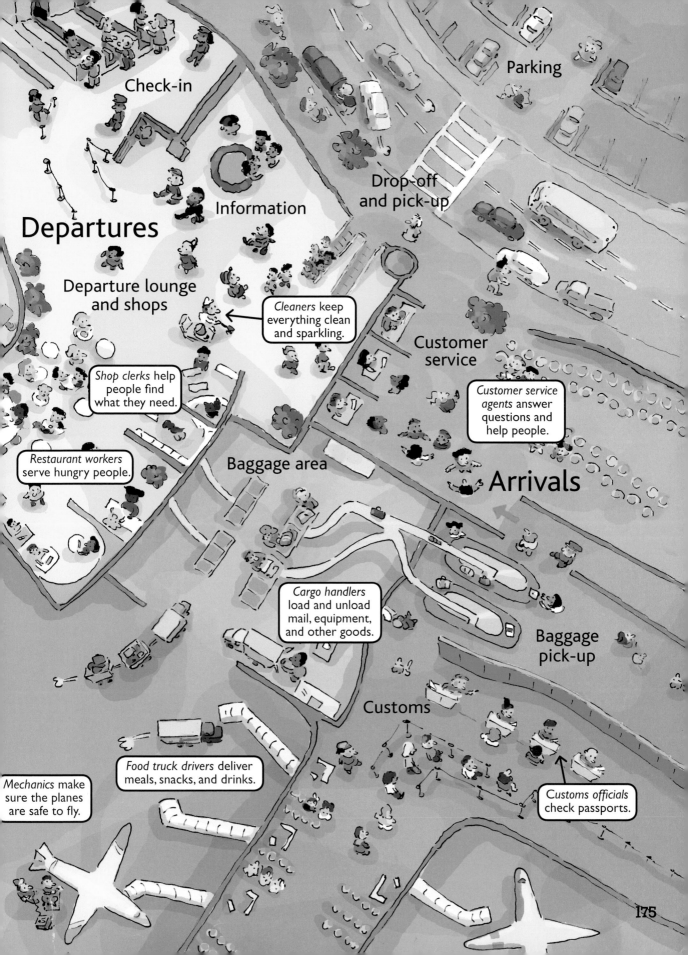

Check-in

Parking

Information

Drop-off and pick-up

Departures

Departure lounge and shops

Cleaners keep everything clean and sparkling.

Customer service

Shop clerks help people find what they need.

Customer service agents answer questions and help people.

Baggage area

Restaurant workers serve hungry people.

Arrivals

Cargo handlers load and unload mail, equipment, and other goods.

Baggage pick-up

Customs

Mechanics make sure the planes are safe to fly.

Food truck drivers deliver meals, snacks, and drinks.

Customs officials check passports.

175

Why do you need a passport?

A passport proves who you are and what country (or countries) you call home. It also gives you the right to return to your home country after you've been traveling. When you want to enter another country, the people at Customs make sure the photo in your passport matches you. They also check the other information, such as the place you were born and your birth date, to make sure you are who you say you are. Passports are very, very important documents, so *bon voyage*, and remember—always keep your passport safe!

How do X-rays work?

X-rays are super at going right through almost any object, and this makes them very useful for looking inside things, such as suitcases, backpacks, and even bodies. Different amounts of X-rays can pass through different objects, and that's what makes the objects look different from one another on the screen. For example, X-rays don't go through metal objects like keys, coins, and golf clubs. Instead these objects take in, or absorb, all the X-rays, which makes their pictures very dark. But a cotton shirt or socks take in very few X-rays because most X-rays travel right through them. The result? Their picture is not as clear and much lighter on the screen.

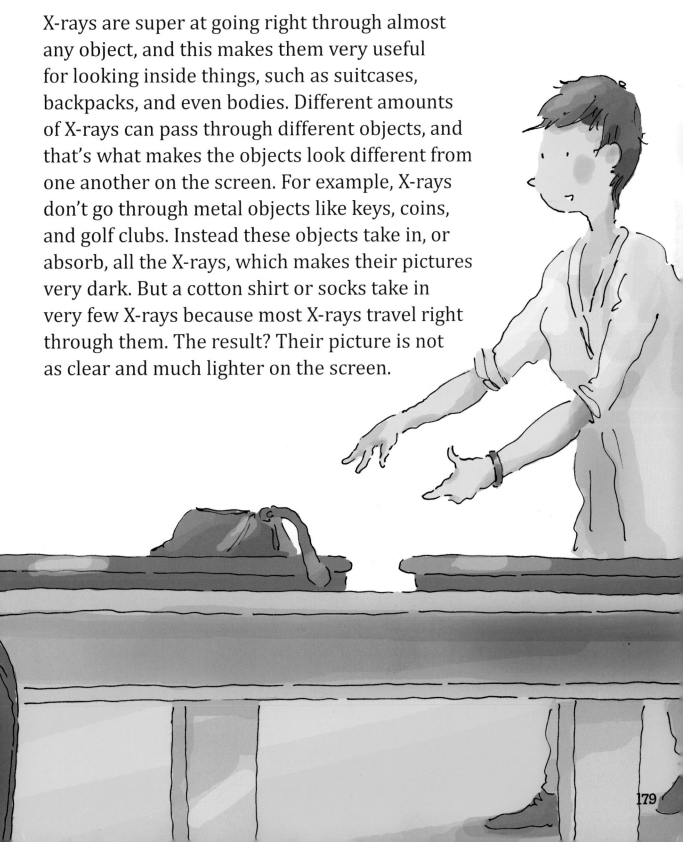

Where does my suitcase go?

From you to the plane and then back to you! When you check in, a tag with a special code is attached to your bag. The code contains information about which flights you are taking. After your bag rolls through the luggage door flaps, it is X-rayed to make sure there is nothing dangerous or against the law inside. A computer scans the tag and sends your suitcase down a ramp to be put on the baggage cart headed for your plane. Then your bag goes up a ramp into the plane. Then guess what? When you land, it all happens in reverse.

Why do hugs make me feel so good?

A warm hug can change what's happening inside your body. When someone you're close to, like your grandma, hugs you, your body makes more of a special substance called oxytocin. More oxytocin in your body helps you trust people and like them more. And that makes you feel great! Also, if you are feeling worried or stressed, a hug can help take away some of your stress. So what are you waiting for? Have you hugged someone special today?

Why does the security gate beep?

Because the person who just walked through the gate is carrying something metal. Here's how it works: Hidden inside the gate is a coil of wire. Electricity pulses through the wire and creates a special force called a magnetic field. Fridge magnets have a magnetic field, too. Just as you can't see the magnetic force that makes a fridge magnet jump toward a metal fridge door, you can't see the magnetic force around the security gate. But it is there, and a metal object going through the gate's magnetic field will set off a loud BEEP!

186

How can planes take off when they weigh so much?

It all has to do with engines, wings, and the air itself. Vro-o-o-o-m...powerful engines zoom the heavy plane forward super fast. This is called thrust. Scho-o-o-m... air speeds over the wings. The special shape of the wings makes the air rush downward, and when the air rushes down, the plane is pushed up. This is called lift. Big, heavy airplanes need big, powerful engines to make the air move really fast. The faster the air moves, the more lift there will be to get the plane off the ground and keep it flying high in the sky.

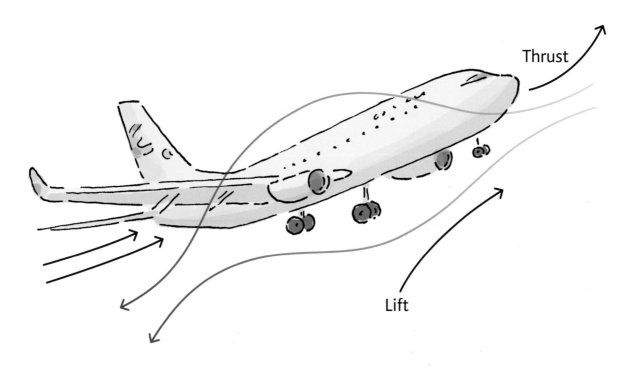

Thrust

Lift

AT THE AIRPORT

Picture of the first flight

Watching planes land and take off

Oma's passport

I can't wait to take a trip.

189

Index

A

air, 17, 79, 99, 100-101, 131, 153, 154, 187
airplanes, 168-169, 170-171, 172
   inventor, 170-171
   landing, 168
   lift, 169, 187
   take-off, 187
   thrust, 187
airport, 168, 172-175
   baggage, 181
   customs, 175, 177
   security, 174, 179, 181, 184
animal shelter, 65
animals
   cats, 76
   dogs, 66-67, 68-69
   fish, 70, 72
   hamsters, 82, 85
   mollusks, 149
   parrots, 79
   pets, 64-65, 82, 85
   seagulls, 146
   snakes, 80
   tarantulas, 75
   vehicles, 135
   whales, 161

B

babies, 25
baking, 26
balloons, 17, 18
beach, 142, 146, 158
benzene, 126
birthday, 15, 21
   gifts, 22
   noisemakers, 21
   party, 15
   song, 28
   superstition, 21
body, 25, 33, 91, 93, 94, 96-97, 99, 103, 109, 132, 149, 153, 182
books, 38, 40, 43-44, 55
   audio, 44
   electronic, 44
   making of, 42-43
brain, 33, 48, 69, 93, 96, 99, 103, 132
breeding, 66
bridges, 124-125
buoyancy, 153

C

cake, 26, 33
calendar, 15
candle, 31
car, 115, 116-117, 128, 132
   inventor, 135
carsick, 93, 132
Cayley, George, 171
cells, 25, 72, 103
cheeks, 85
computers, 44, 51, 52-53, 58, 181
   CDs, 53

   memory, 53
   programming, 52
cough, 101, 103, 105
Cugnot, Nicolas, 135
currents, 157

D

doctor, 94, 104-105
dreaming, 68-69
droplets, 101
dry, 141, 145

E

Earth, 131, 154, 158
eggs, 26, 39
electricity, 184
energy, 103, 115, 157
engines, 187
eyes, 72, 133

F

fever, 91, 96-97, 109
fibers, 18
fire, 31, 126
floating, 153
force, 153, 184

G

gases, 17, 26, 31, 128
   carbon dioxide, 17, 26
   chlorine, 154
   helium, 17
   natural, 126
   smell, 126
   water vapor, 154
gasoline, 126
gears, 115, 168
germs, 91, 93, 96-97, 100-101, 103, 105, 109
   in the air, 100-101
   bacteria, 93, 109
   on surfaces, 100-101
   viruses, 93, 105
gifts, 22
gravity, 153

H

hairs, 75
health, 104-105
  medicine, 109
  resting, 103
  sick, 91, 93, 96, 103, 104,
    109, 132
  sound, 76
  temperature, 94, 96-97, 105
heat, 26, 31, 94, 96-97, 126,
  131, 141
height, 25
Hill sisters, 28
hugs, 182

I

intelligence, 48
internet, 51, 53
inventions
  airplane, 171
  birthday song, 28
  car, 135
  library, 38
  wheel, 119

J

jaws, 80

L

laboratory, 106
librarians, 40, 55
library, 38
  books, 38, 40-41, 55
  borrowing, 38, 40, 51, 58
  call numbers, 55
  catalog, 51
  checkout system, 58
  collection, 40
  computers, 44, 51, 52-53
  quiet, 47
  restroom, 57
light, 72, 131

M

magnetic field, 184
magnets, 184
mantle (mollusks), 149

medicine, 106, 109
melanin, 163
metal, 179, 184
microbes, 91, 106
microscope, 18, 91
mirage, 131
Moon, 15, 158
mucus, 103
muscles, 93, 96, 99

O

ocean, 72, 142, 154
  tides, 158
  waves, 157
  whales, 161
oven, 26
oxytocin, 182

P

paper, 22
passport, 177
pet stores, 65
pollution, 128, 161
printing press, 22
public buildings, 57
purring, 76

R

rays, 131, 141, 163
reading, 48, 132
roads, 120-123, 124, 128, 131
  speed limit, 128
  traffic signs, 116-117
round, 119
running, 82
runway, 168, 174

S

salt, 154
salt water, 154
sand, 141, 142, 145
sandcastles, 145, 158
seashells, 142, 149, 150
seasons, 15
skin, 94, 132, 163
sleep, 68-69

smell, 33, 72, 126
sneezing, 99, 101, 103
sodium, 154
sound
  birds, 79
  cats, 76
  seashells, 150
  waves, 150
speed, 128
stomach, 93, 99
sugar, 26, 33
Sun, 15, 131, 141, 158, 163
sunburn, 163

T

taste, 33, 75
territory, 70
tides, 146, 158

U

ultraviolet rays, 163

V

vomit, 93

W

water, 141, 142, 145, 154,
157, 158
  buoyancy, 153
  vapor, 154
wax, 31
wheels, 82, 115, 119
wick, 31
wind, 142, 150, 157
Wright brothers, 171

X

X-ray, 179, 181

Acknowledgments

First, for 839 super questions. Thank you to the children at Brookside, Duggan, Elmwood, George P. Nicholson, Keheewin, Lansdowne, Oliver, Pollard Meadows, Princeton, and Richard Secord schools, whom I visited in Spring 2010, for their questions, and thank you to their teachers and principals for their gracious welcome. Thanks, too, to Cheryl Miller, who came along and took notes, and to Dr. John Mcnab, Research Consultant, Edmonton Public Schools, who set it all up for me.

Second, for help with the answers. Thank you to the following experts who advised on my draft answers, for which I take full responsibility: John H. Acorn, Department of Renewable Resources, University of Alberta; Rex Banks, Chief Audiologist & Director, Hearing Healthcare, The Canadian Hearing Society; Wallace P. Bolen, United States Geological Survey; Dr. Randall Brooks, Canada Science and Technology Museum; Dr. Barry Burtis, Bay Cities Animal Hospital, Burlington, ON; Dr. C. Sue Carter, The Brain Body Center, University of Illinois at Chicago; Katena Carvajales, Hartfield-Jackson Atlanta International Airport; Dr. Howard Chudacoff, Brown University; Dr. Brian Coad, Research, Canadian Museum of Nature; Consulting Services, Edmonton Public Schools; Sarah Cox, Edmonton International Airport; Dr. Rénald Fortier, Canada Aviation and Space Museum; Michel Gosselin, Collection Services, Canadian Museum of Nature; Stephen King, PCL Construction Management Inc.; Dennis S. Kostick, United States Geological Survey; Rob Lane, Municipal Affairs, Government of Alberta; Dr. Michelle Levy, Department of Family Medicine, University of Alberta; Dr. André Martel, Research, Canadian Museum of Nature; Tom Mason, Curator of Invertebrates & Birds, Metro Toronto Zoo; Louis McCann, Executive Director, Pet Industry Joint Advisory Council of Canada; Steve Otto, Alberta Transportation; Dr. William Perrin, National Oceanic and Atmospheric Administration; Atison Phumchoosri, Thailand; Pam Pritchard, Animal Collection Specialist, Calgary Zoo; Véronique Robitaille, Passport Canada/Passeport Canada; Kimberly Reynolds, Canada Aviation and Space Museum; Tamsin Shute, Librarian (Youth Services), Edmonton Public Libraries; Dr. Doug Whiteside, Calgary Zoo; and Dr. George Zahariadis, Alberta Health Services.

Third, for all the creativity and support from Owlkids. Thank you to Mary Beth for the phone call, the opportunity, and her guidance; to John, who also contributed in this role; to my editors, Anne and Katherine, for their questions, suggestions, and patience; to Barb for leading the visual side with zip and imagination; and of course...to Scot, who once again has brought such fun, warmth, and love to every page.

Last but not least, thank you to my ever-curious Bruce, who, amazingly, still loves me after 30-plus years. This one's for you!